A Dog's Life:
Boomer Jack of the Northwestern Pacific

by Lincoln Kilian

Funding provided by Grassroots History Publications of Mendocino County Museum

Grassroots History Publication Number 18

Printed by Eureka Printing Company, Inc.
Eureka, California

Original book design and typography by Rebecca Snetselaar

First Edition 1998
Second Edition 1999
Third Edition 2005

ISBN 0-9748934-3-9
LCCN 2004109073

For Leila, from her grandfather

"BOOMER JACK"
N. W. P. MASCOT

Photo, c. 1916, from engineer Andy Kirkpatrick's trunk.
Courtesy of Robert Brantley.

Boomer Jack was a bob-tailed dog, just under medium size. Some remember him as black, others say dark brown. His ancestry was anyone's guess: terrier, lab and shepherd were suggested – all, perhaps, with some accuracy. He was friendly enough, yet there remained about him a certain reserve, an unmistakable sense that he was his own dog. "He may have been a mutt," says a woman who knew him well, "but he was also an aristocrat."

Jack rode railroad trains. We will probably never know just how or where he chose his career, since history seldom bothers with stray dogs before they've proven themselves. But he must have set out as a pup, for his recorded life spans almost a dog's age.

No one recalls where Boomer Jack was on October 23, 1914 – a momentous date in his life. On that day Warren S. Palmer, President of the Northwestern Pacific Railroad, drove a golden spike into a redwood tie at Cain Rock in

The Cain Rock golden spike ceremony, Oct. 23, 1914. NWP president W.S. Palmer and his daughter Alice in the foreground. Photo by E.R. Freeman.

Courtesy of Humboldt State University Library, HSU Photo #1596

the remote southeastern corner of Humboldt County, California. Then, as hundreds cheered, his pretty daughter Alice smashed a bottle of California champagne against the rail, which now stretched 300 unbroken miles between the San Francisco and Humboldt Bay regions.

The NWP was a creation of the Southern Pacific and the Santa Fe railroads, former rivals joining forces to tackle the costliest track-laying job in history: one hundred mountainous miles between Willits and Shively. Only after $13 million, 30 tunnels, and countless tons of fill did Mr. Palmer swing his silver maul.

By this time Jack was almost certainly in business – at which end of the line isn't clear. Train master R.D. Shugrue, who worked at Santa Rosa in 1912 and '13, remembers, "a short-haired, black mongrel...between 35 and 40 pounds" riding the engines, but never learned his name.

Eileen Christopher, daughter of a station

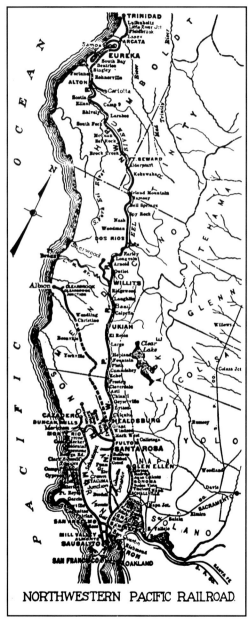

NORTHWESTERN PACIFIC RAILROAD.

agent at Humboldt Bay, insists that Boomer Jack called on her family during the same years. Maybe <u>both</u> of these dogs were Jack: a bumpy dirt highway connected Willits and Shively before 1914, and he was known to commandeer anything that moved, even when no trains were handy.

Whatever his origins, the conquest of northwestern California by rail created for

Boomer Jack a vast private empire, which he toured at whim aboard mighty steam engines for the rest of his life. He took his name from the "boomers" – freelance railroad workers who drifted from town to town (some called him "Hobo Jack" or "Bummer Jack"). He had no master, but hundreds of protectors – the engineers, firemen, brake-

Corrected to May 25 1924

Northwestern Pacific Railroad Company

Time Tables
(Except Interurban)

"Vacation, 1924"

This illustrated descriptive booklet contains authoritative information on more than 150 resorts in the territory served by the Northwestern Pacific Railroad. It will assist you in selecting your summer outing place. Copies may be had free of cost at 712 Market Street, or Ferry Ticket Office; or by writing to J. J. Geary, General Passenger Agent, 64 Pine Street, San Francisco, California.

5-19-24-30M
Printed in U.S.A.

men, conductors, switchmen, sectionmen, mechanics, and station agents of the Northwestern Pacific.

Jack's lifestyle was simple in theory; he ranged back and forth between Humboldt and Marin counties, stopping off at stations or trainmen's homes. But his actual schedule was unpredictable. Lois Watson, whose father ran the station at Essex, remembers he might show up on any train, lounge around for a few hours to a day or two, then be off again for a day or a month. All agree he was very particular in choosing his hosts. Engineer Bob McNeil recalls how privileged he felt the few times Jack deigned to follow him home and sleep on his porch.

In Eureka, many trainmen lived far from the station, so Jack visited them by streetcar. He learned the routes and shuttled back and forth on his own – no great feat, apparently, for a railroad dog. Ray Haley, who ran a trolley from

Streetcar line, 5th Street near F. Street in Eureka, California, 1909.
Courtesy of Humboldt State University Library, HSU Photo #2291.

1913 to 1916, still remembers the freeloading passenger.

Sustenance was no problem for Boomer Jack. Aside from the extra morsels specially packed in trainmen's lunches, and the bounty from his overnight hosts, he cased every restaurant along the route. In Eureka he frequented the alleys behind Young's Restaurant and Abe's Chop House, awaiting his accustomed scraps.

Alley where Boomer Jack often mooched his meals, between 1st and 2nd Streets, looking south from C Street, in Eureka, California, 1923.
Courtesy of Humboldt State University Library, HSU Photo #460.

In Arcata, according to Station Clerk Blanche Buck, he usually made the round of eateries in early afternoon, returning in time to pick and choose among the late-departing trains. If an establishment was the rougher type that catered to workingmen, Jack simply strode in the front door, sniffed out a railroader – even a stranger – from among the rows of loggers, teamsters and farm hands, and sat directly behind him in expectation of tribute.

When on the move Jack rode in the engine cab, usually on the back of the engineer's seat-box. When he wanted to enjoy the scenery he hopped on the fireman's seat and stuck his head and front paws out the window. There were, inevitably, one or two grumpy engineers who didn't want a dog in their cab. He tried to avoid them, but when he couldn't he retired discreetly to the caboose or baggage car.

Boomer Jack's only actual run-in with a railroader occurred early in his career, when he called on a female dog owned by a Mrs. Sappingfield, wife of the agent at South Fork. The resentful woman dumped a pot of boiling water on Jack's back, near his stub of a tail. A storm of indignation swept the usually placid village as his many friends hurried to the rescue. Tempers eventually cooled and Jack recovered, but for the rest of his life he bore a round patch of discolored hair over the battle-scar. This little fracas aside, his reception everywhere was friendly and admiring – more so as his fame grew. The <u>Humboldt Times</u> of July 22, 1918 described a typical stopover:

"...Jack is the well known and much loved mascot of the trainmen, a small black bob-tailed terrier and is welcome whenever and wherever he chooses to visit. He has a free pass on every freight train on the road. He left his train at Eel Rock Monday evening, enjoyed a refreshing bath in the river, inspected the track and station, visited the schoolchildren and talked impartially to each and every one, and accepted several dinner invitations. He is a great favorite with all the little folks and fares well at their hands. Finding everything to his satisfaction, he en-trained on the next freight. Any place in the road where Jack chooses he may flag a train by simply waiting in the middle of the track. He boards the engine via the cowcatcher and fender

Northwestern Pacific depot at South Fork, c. 1920.
Courtesy of Peter E. Palmquist Collection, Beinecke Rare Book and Manuscript Library, Yale University.

and finds a certain welcome awaiting him in the caboose. He chooses his own domicile at all times and it is the lucky crew that has the honor of carrying him."

Braking a steam engine wasn't easy, so it's doubtful Jack really "waited in the middle of the track." Nor was he limited to freights, as the story implies; he often rode passenger trains.

Another story, probably from the <u>Blue Lake</u> <u>Advocate</u>, records a more rigorous episode:

"...One fine day at the Blue Lake Depot, Boomer was having such a happy time with his local canine friends that he neglected to notice the departure of the down train. It wasn't long before he realized that he had missed the train, for he was soon tearing after it with desperate efforts. Boomer may have been a sponger, but when necessity compelled him to exert himself, he was equal to the demand. He followed the train nearly to Glendale. Engineer Sundquist happened to see him panting over the long trestle by the Glendale schoolhouse and waited for him at the Glendale station."

Emma Smith of Shively has spent her life beside the right-of-way. She knows nothing of Jack's life, she says, but does recall the shouts among her playmates whenever he approached, and joining in their dash to the tracks to watch him soar by, ears flapping in the wind, half out

Shively, California, 1910.
Courtesy of Peter E. Palmquist Collection, Beinecke Rare Book and Manuscript Library, Yale University.

the window of a roaring locomotive.

The NWP operated in two geographic worlds, its Northern and Southern Divisions, centered at the Mendocino County town of Willits. Just north of Willits rose the rugged, forested terrain so recently subdued by the track-gangs. The railroad clung to the sides of the winding Eel River Canyon, where floods and landslides constantly plagued operations. This was redwood country: such "towns" as existed were mostly crude lumber camps where snorting "steam donkeys" hauled trunks to the railway, and where a pair of loggers might chop and saw for two days to fell a single tree. Beyond the Eel the line traversed the lush farmlands of the Humboldt Bay area, ending at the coastal village of Trinidad.

South of Willits stretched the classic California landscape of Mendocino, Sonoma and Marin Counties – rolling green hills and oak trees, vineyards and orchards, poultry farms and dairy pastures. The rails ended at Sausalito, where NWP ferries embarked across the Golden Gate to San Francisco.

Jack's friends sometimes took him on the ferry for a look at big-city life. On one such visit a trainman smuggled him into his hotel room. The management somehow – through a tactless bark, perhaps – discovered the unregistered guest and ejected both man and dog from the

TRANSFER OF PASSENCERS AROUND SLIDE ON SCOTIA BLUFF KEIENº 635

Transfer of passengers around a landslide at the Scotia
Bluffs, c. 1920.
*Courtesy of Peter E. Palmquist Collection, Beinecke Rare Book and
Manuscript Library, Yale University.*

premises. Soon afterwards, Jack and his friends
were walking through the same neighborhood
when suddenly he turned through the hotel
door to the lobby, raised his leg against the
nearest piece of furniture, and strolled out
again.

The San Francisco excursions apparently
aroused Jack's curiosity about the wider world,

Ferry "Tamalpais" leaving the slip at Sausalito; the "Marin" is tied up to the pier, c. 1925.

Courtesy of the Northwestern Pacific Railroad Historical Society, Ted Wurm Collection, #90.002.0123.

leading to his greatest adventure. He never an-
nounced his intentions, but one day simply
vanished. As weeks went by his worried friends
realized that he wasn't appearing at his usual
stops – that no one had seen him anywhere.
They began to fear the worst. Then a telegram
arrived at company headquarters from some
trainmen in South Carolina. It said, in effect,
"There's a dog running around here with an
NWP badge on his collar. Do you know anything
about him?" The Northwesterners, immensely
relieved, figured out the best connections for his
return and wired back instructions. And so the
wayward Boomer Jack was passed hand to
hand by railroad men across America, all the
way back to his home line. The details of his
journey east remained a mystery, but he must
have begun it by stowing away on the ferry to
San Francisco, the nearest hub of eastbound
traffic.

He returned, wiser and more famous, to his

old haunts. He was in his prime. A photo of the young Boomer Jack has turned up in a dusty trunk once owned by engineer Andy Kirkpatrick, who died in 1954. The dog in the blurred picture looks sleek and alert. Perhaps a spark of his uncanny intelligence, described by all who knew him, comes through as well.

On July 3, 1920, Jack was headed south to celebrate the Fourth at Ukiah when he spotted something – a deer or a rabbit – from the window, just as the engine jolted around a curve. He leaned out a little too far, and tumbled from the cab. The distraught crew couldn't stop in time to help, so they scribbled a note, attached it to a signal, and dropped it for the next section gang that happened by. The gang found him badly bruised and bleeding, his left foreleg broken, and carefully carried him the few miles north to Willits.

He languished there for a month. The most tender nursing by his friends didn't seem to help. Fearing they might lose him, they issued a call up and down the line; send money – Boomer Jack needs professional care. His arrival by train in Eureka on the 30th was headlined in local papers. At Doctor Rolley's veterinary hospital he finally rallied, and became almost his old self again. The call for funds raised far more than enough – so much more that his friends opened an account for him at a Eureka bank. Never again did Jack have to worry about a vet bill.

The lameness never left his leg, and he wasn't getting any younger. He began to slow down a bit, and spent more time curled behind the wood stove in every station. Mrs. Buck, the clerk at Arcata, has found a photo of him in her family album, taken around 1923. He's a little heavier than before, a little more grizzled. But it never occurred to him to quit. As more years went by he became too old and stiff to jump into an engine. But when he picked out a train and

Boomer Jack with Ben Vaissade and Blanche Buck at the
Arcata NWP station, c. 1923.
Courtesy of Blanche Buck.

waited quietly on the platform a crewman would lift him gently into the cab. "What you have to understand," says retired conductor Claude Pinches, "is how much we loved that old dog."

Although he may not have known it, Jack was not just a lone vagabond but – by this time – the venerable successor to a long tradition of American railroad dogs. Many of the notables are chronicled by Freeman Hubbard in his treasure of rail lore, Railroad Avenue. There was Owney of the Railway Post Office, who circled the world in the 1890s; Roxie of the Long Island RR, who toured the East for 12 years and knew Teddy Roosevelt; Admiral Dewey of the New York, New Haven & Hartford, who covered 50,000 miles in three years. There was Railroad Jack of the New York Central, Paddy of the Camas Prairie, Little Hop of the Nashville, Chattanooga & St. Louis, Santa Fe Jack, and many more. Of this distinguished group Boomer Jack was a paragon. Few could match him for independence (most actually belonged to a train-man) or length of service – at least 14 years. His total mileage in every direction almost defies reckoning.

Bob Brown hired on as a boilermaker at the Willits roundhouse in June of 1926. It was the following summer, as best he recalls, that he and his shopmates arrived at work one day to find Boomer Jack lying dead at the door of the station office. He looked peaceful and unmarked – just ran out of steam, they figured. Bob collected some redwood scraps from a nearby mill, then helped nail together a small coffin. They buried Jack in the switchyard, between the arms of a Y in the tracks, and raised a wooden cross over his grave. Word spread quickly, and many friends came by for a last farewell.

Soon after Jack's death the Southern Pacific took over sole ownership of the NWP. The first diesel engine appeared in the mid-30s. Twenty years later the age of steam was history.

Boomer Jack's grave, Willits, California, c. 1927. Fred Nelson, roundhouse foreman, fourth from the right; Marlon Fauerbaugh, section crew foreman, third from the right.
Courtesy of Mrs. Beatrice Mavey, widow of conductor Budd Mavey.

The Christmas floods of 1964 destroyed nearly a hundred miles of track – one of America's worst railroad disasters. After a huge repair job the gold spike of 1914 was brought to South Fork for the reopening ceremony.

Today the modern diesels of the Northwestern Pacific still rumble through the wine country and the redwood forests – and past the grave of Boomer Jack.

ABOUT THE AUTHOR

Born and raised in Los Angeles, Lincoln Kilian spent a nomadic early life in Mexico City, British Columbia, and Berkeley. In 1966 he moved to Humboldt County, California, where he earned a B.A. in Social Science from Humboldt State University, and joined the University Library staff. He first learned of Boomer Jack in 1979, from an undated clipping in the Library's Humboldt County Collection. Then, after a fruitless search of current sources, spent the next two years scanning unindexed newspaper backfiles, and tracking down the last surviving old-timers who remembered the railroad dog.

Lincoln Kilian co-authored, with the late Peter Palmquist, a series of seven volumes entitled The Photographers of the Humboldt Bay Region.

Recently retired, Mr. Kilian lives with his cat in a small cabin in the woods near Trinidad, California.